SHADOW SOUNDS

For Georgette

It's so nice having such a "fun" colleague + friend who even has more energy and interests than I do.

I hope you enjoy the book

Jan

Shadow Sounds

Poems by

Joan Kantor

Antrim House
Simsbury, Connecticut

Copyright © 2010 by Joan B. Kantor

Except for short selections reprinted for purposes of
book review, all reproduction rights are reserved.
Requests for permission to replicate should
be addressed to the publisher.

Library of Congress Control Number: 2010928378

ISBN: 978-0-9843418-1-8

Printed & bound by United Graphics, Inc.

First Edition, 2010

Front cover (*Glorious Marshlands,* photo collage):
Lori Barker and Joan Kantor

Author photograph by Gail Stanton

Photographs pp. 17, 41 by Sheldon Gants

Photographs pp. 13, 69, 89 by Daniel Kantor

Image p. 105: *L'Écoute by* Henri de Miller

Cover Design by Joan Kantor

Book design by Rennie McQuilkin

Antrim House
860.217.0023
AntrimHouse@comcast.net
www.AntrimHouseBooks.com
21 Goodrich Road, Simsbury, CT 06070

Preface

This book is the culmination of a joyful writing life. I can still remember the thrill of my first words of poetry: *The bunny stopped. He went hop hop hop.* You have to start somewhere! My life and poetry have been inextricably entwined, feeding each other constantly. Poems pour forth spontaneously, almost effortlessly, and then the work begins. Each poem is crafted, rebuilt and fine-tuned countless times in a labor of love. Poetry is too often inscrutable; I strive to make mine, though thoughtful, clear and accessible. I want to share my appreciation of the world's beauty and also the way struggles and hardships, those shadow sounds, add perspective and depth to life. Most importantly, however, this book is a legacy for my children, who have contributed so much to my life and work.

Thanks to Cheryl and Gail for their support and for carefully listening to my work, to Tere Foley for being my first "partner in poetry," and to Peterson Toscano for his thoughtful contributions. Also, special thanks to Rennie McQuilkin, not only for his extraordinary editing skills, but for his respect, honesty, enthusiasm and patience. He made the experience of creating my book both an education and a joy.

Joan B. Kantor
Collinsville, CT
May 3, 2010

To Chuck
who continues to be more than I could ever have asked for.
Without his encouragement, this book
wouldn't exist.

Table of Contents

PROLOGUE

Word Soup / 3
All-Nighter / 4

BECOMING

Moving On / 7
Summer Escape / 9
All Hallows Eve / 10
Reality Rites / 11
Tangled Roots / 13
Impossible / 15
The Hunt / 17
Threatened / 19
Tasting the Fruit of the Vine / 20
On the Edge / 22
Shock / 23
Ride of a Lifetime / 25
In Touch / 26
Becoming Her / 27

WITNESS

Temptation / 31
Offerings / 32
The Air Show / 33
Burnt / 34
Autumn Marsh / 35
Autumn Eve's Chill / 36
Late September / 37
Assault / 38
Seen Through the Eye of a Storm / 39
To Finally Fall / 40

Under the Surface / 41
Exposed / 42
River Rodeo / 43
Germination / 44
Before the Picnic / 45
Witness / 46
Misnomer under "Odonata" / 47
Breakfast Tide / 48
Awakening / 49
Motion Picture / 50
Beavers at Bantam / 51
The Find / 53
My Jungle / 55
The Point / 56

TO BE THERE

Confused in Collinsville / 59
Steam Room Reverie / 60
Homesteading / 61
Just Another Intermission / 63
Newsworthy / 64
Ending a New York Love Affair / 65
City Roots / 67
Before the Feast / 68
Through Brussels to Bruegel / 70
Byzantine Eyes / 72
Bartholomew's Cobble / 73
Jumieges / 74
Asana / 75

OTHER LIVES

Words for an Abuser / 79
Through the Wringer / 80
Worlds Removed / 81
Bringing Her Back / 82

Round and Round / 83
Friday after School / 84
They Will Be Watching / 85
Their Turn / 86
Almost / 87
Tuned into the Harp / 88
Misjudging Jo / 90
More than a Boss / 91

FAMILIAR FACES

The Potter's Hands / 95
To Be Clay / 97
When We Communed / 98
Best Week of the Year / 99
He Found a Way / 102
After the Funeral / 105
To Be Heard / 106
The Hug / 107
In My 45th Year / 109
She Was / 110
Miriam / 112
Mother-in-Law / 113
The Circle / 115
His Morning Detail / 116
The Affair / 120
For Isabella / 122
Selective Memories / 124
Now That He's Back / 126
Salt on Ice / 129
Leah's Timeless Face / 130
As It Must Be / 131

ABOUT THE AUTHOR / 133

"Suffering has been stronger than all other teaching and has taught me to understand... I have been bent and broken, but–I hope–into a better shape." – Charles Dickens, GREAT EXPECTATIONS

"The dew seemed to sparkle more brightly on the green leaves; the air to rustle among them with a sweeter music; and the sky itself to look more blue and bright. Such is the influence which the condition of our own thoughts, exercise, even over the appearance of external objects." – Charles Dickens, OLIVER TWIST

Word Soup

It's what I do

soup and words

Poems and potage
spring from my mind

bits of this and that
tossed in the pot
or on the page
It's all the same

I feel the warmth

of words
stirring together

my hand
firmly
on the spoon

All-Nighter

In college
I never pulled all-nighters

With advancing middle age
they've become a way of life

Twisting and tossing
blankets and sheets
overwhelmed by the heat

I futilely open
windows and doors
trying to cool off

then hopelessly
head downstairs
where ideas and words
stumble and fall
into the net of a poem

that in the morning
though true
sounds wrong

and I work and play
half awake
fine-tuning
what sleeplessness wrought

hoping
that tonight
my writing
will hold off
until daylight

Moving On

His training wheels
rattle the ground
and the sound
seeps
into my marrow

The mantra
of pebble-jogged rubber
on pavement
sloughs off
my grownup skin

And I'm back in my hometown
under the tree
The macadam circle is mine

as I grind out
my message
with off-balance wheels

Ready
Set
Go

Reluctantly
Daddy removes nuts and bolts

Props fall
and I swallow my breath

loving the fear
I wait for his push

    He holds back

        Tension snaps

and I fly

Summer Escape

I lived
for sand-worn bottle glass
frosty or clear

School was fear
filtering out the light

Summertime was safety

Boardwalk splinters
stabbed my feet
but I didn't care

The pinball games
were worth the pain
played between licks
of lemon ice

while drinking in
the ring-a-dings
of my favorite baseball game

Touching sand-worn bottle glass
smooth blue
emerald
gold and red

I thought
summer
would never end

All Hallows Eve

Gates
     loose on hinges
slap
      at the dark

Ice vapor ghosts
          swirl from mouths

Bats and skeletons
         dangle
              from trees
Thoughts
     of footsteps
        are
           chasing
              us
                 home

Reality Rites

Subway fingers
stretched their way
out to seashore suburbs
rattling our bones
and dusting shelves
with soot

but we were safe
at home
with backyard barbecues
the beach
and boardwalk

the ocean
cradling us
in blankets of salt air

till one day
a body was found

Our imaginings
followed us
through days
and into nightmares

Parents
kept silent
sparing us truth

only scolding
"Stay close to home!"

But we
had to see
for ourselves

I'm not sure
if I ever really looked
or just saw
through the eyes
of friends

the fetal-folded imprint
in the weeds
of the vacant lot
next to the store

whose jingle
rang hollow

School bells ring
and children sing
It's back
to Robert Hall
again

I never went back

Tangled Roots

Over the river
and through the woods
I can't find my grandparents' house

I long for my roots
but nobody knows
or chooses to tell

My father's father
was loving and gruff
That's all

His mother
died young
leaving holes

She was perfect
a saint
I need more

My mother's mother
bore six children
Sweet
simple
she never shared

My mother's father
lost in sadness
was almost not there

She never once
saw them kiss

His sadness
ended
in the East River

I want
my questions
answered

but all that's left
for me

are tangled roots

Impossible

She was the favored one
till she wasn't anymore

Adorable
extrovert
she was a star

I was shy
with hidden gifts
I whined and cried
to be noticed

They showed her off

denying me

When we got older
she floundered in school
and I was the star

They bragged about me

diminishing her

I was the selfish one
till one day she was

We were never sure
whose turn
it would be

and spent childhood
hoping
yet failing

to please

The Hunt

Stalking my prey
in shops
and craft shows

on the hunt
I go for the kill

adding
vibrant colors
textures
shapes

to my wardrobe

No antlers
on the walls
I wear my trophies
all week long

I feed
off constant change

shopping
over and over
again

I indulge myself
in the guise
of artistic expression

But it's never enough

I wear things once
and then move on

I hunt
in vain
to fill closets
already too full

The emptiness
must be
somewhere else

    Communal arms
               held me
in the hum
      of familiar chants

And when my son began
his reading from The Torah
the modern sanctuary
became an ancient shul

The shaven men
grew beards
and wore long robes

On the Edge

My belly sinkhole
swallows life
stealing hunger pangs

What's left
is a vague remembrance of joy

Isolation
mocks me

It peels off my mask
and settles its hollow ache
in my gut

My body recoils
from the jagged edges
of sleep

Loved ones
reach out soothingly

and teetering
on the edge
I stretch

to barely
feel their touch

Shock

I'm desperate

Everything's
been tried

The heaviness
weighs me down

I choose to
relinquish myself

to what
used to be
called
barbaric

They call
my name

Familiar smiles
greet me

Soon their faces
loom
from above

I long
for what
I don't want

but need

The drip begins

The passage
of time
disappears

I awaken
to a different
world

once heavy
now light

once clear
now fog

Someone
guides me
by the hand

takes me home

where
for weeks
I lie low

waiting
for life
and memory

to return

Ride of a Lifetime

Unexpected
with voluptuous roar
thundering
the dam breaks

and the river
forever held back
is rushing
seizing
branches and leaves

sucking my craft
into a vortex

where
lost memories
spinning
fall
to the bottom

and shadow sounds
meet their end

Suddenly
wild water
spits me free

and running
its rapids

I dig my paddle
into a torrent
of poems

In Touch

As shadow sounds lurk
I pull my strokes
through depths
of hidden water

Alive with the moon
I am
my surroundings

Those who fear water snakes
won't understand
why I've sought
this place

Though untamed
unleashed
I see my calm reflection

The night
holds no threat
for me

Becoming Her

There was a woman
I greatly admired

She was caring
creative
self-confident
daring

She was smart
and had a career

She completed herself
as a wife
and mother

while I cowered
and cringed
filled with fear

For me
risks
weren't an option

Then
I began

The process
was slow

but I'd married
a man
who believed
in my growth

My children
were the challenging kind
and mothering them
made me stronger

I went back to school
found a job
that I love

I have friends
who are like sisters

Words flow
joyously
from my pen

In the mirror
I now
see her

WITNESS

Temptation

I won't be fooled by the softness
of slow motion
swirls

folding
their whiteness
into
the batter
of night

A gossamer confection

To take a taste
would be to join
the ghosts
that suck me under

Offerings

Bearing
      the imprint
            of waters
                  and wind
        marsh grasses
              matted
                  and swirled
offer bowls
        full of
            chartreuse
                and shadow

The Air Show

Thousands of swallows
flying as one

are changing color

shape

wings opening
closing

black
to white

in perfect rhythm
catching wind

Venetian blinds
in flight

Burnt

Thick with sod
before the crisping

summer's sponge
beneath my feet
plush green

till August

burns
each blade
to brown

Autumn Marsh

Salt marsh straws
sucked dry of green

are matted down
like scruffy hair

cowlick-spiked
unruly drab

against the earth's broad scalp

Autumn Eve's Chill

Gusting
      from nowhere

winter's hint
    ripples the surface
          of silence

In a split-second race
        leftover light
           sails
              on a shiver of waves

to suddenly
sink
into stillness

Late September

Peach and gold
on tiptoes of red
prance across the treetops

Making merry
    the dance of death
they bring joy
to fading green
aglow
    in a gilded
        crimson
            finale
November's bare branches
unseen

Assault

Raindrops
        suspended
from rails
           on the deck
sway
    as scrub pines
             slow-dance
to the pulse
        of crooning
                salt wind
     till the hurricane
            swallowing calm
                  slams ashore
forcing windsongs
          into howls
                snapping elastic trees
speeding
      the domino fall
               of marsh grass
slicing air
      with dune-stolen sand

Seen Through the Eye of a Storm

The candle glows
    its hazy hollow

into a backdrop
    of blindness

Silence

snuffs out
the world

We sit still
    full of fear
and excitement

awaiting the storm's
    second half

Fumbling fingers
in flickering light

are seeking
to switch on the known

The strength
of the storm
cuts umbilical cord

By the warmth
    of the flame
we are humbled

To Finally Fall

    Stand quietly

Listen

    The tinkling of snow

        is tapping on oak leaves
            of autumn's neglect

The weight
    will unhinge them

        to finally fall

Under the Surface

at Roaring Brook Nature Center

Suspended motion
        crackled in ice
glitters
   on the stream
Bubbles
    pressed up
        against canopy glass
zigzagging
     gurgle through snares
till finally
      water
         spills out
            over stones
splashing freedom
        on snow-covered banks

Exposed

The river's roiling

Sun's melting snow

Though I long
for warm weather

the transformation
chills

I've been safe
in my seasonal shell

with books
and hearth

where winter weight
hides
in billowing clothes

I let
teasing hints
of summer
taunt

and freeze

at the thought
of being exposed

River Rodeo

Riding
      on riffles

and bucked
      by waves

reflections
      of trees
            and sky
rise
  and
    fall
slapping
    into
        stone saddles

Germination

Seed pearls
        sewn
                on dandelion veils
release themselves
        to the wind

where they swing and sway
                      in downward drift
                                  towards earth

Before the Picnic

A hazy blanket
        of budding chartreuse
is flavoring air
        with green
spreading the table
        for summer

Witness

Calm
beyond the mating dance
of honks
and flapping wings

the sated geese
glide on the pond
energy
all spent

Knowing
they have just performed

their eyes
confide
in me

Misnomer Under "Odonata"

Nature likes to hide itself. – Heraclitis

From slimy brown molting nymph
your rainbow rotors rise newborn
from water plants and muck
to conjure up false cues
of stingers
stuck in tender flesh

Like whirring helicopter blades
your buzzing wings
make people cringe
from violet-emerald hues

till lightly you descend
upon a nearby leaf
and silently
Tiffany translucence
lacy-veined
reminds us
that all dragonflies
are damsels

Odonata: the order of insects that includes dragonflies and damselflies

Breakfast Tide

Morning
    has lifted
        the silver-blue
            covers of tide

stranding
    pools
        of life
            in mud
where snowy egrets
    stabbing food
        puncture
            their reflections

Gulls
    in downward
        gentle flight
know there is no rush
to choose
    from the buffet
        exposed below

Awakening

Wisps of wind
    tickle the air

stirring leaves
    from summer sleep

skimming the lake
    swaying in steam

sifting through screens
    setting curtains aswirl

brushing
    soggy
        half asleep souls

Forerunner of thunder
    soon lightning will fly

and rain
    will awaken the world

Motion Picture

Rippling reflections
        flash from the stream

Projecting motion
        translucent sunshadows
flickering glitter
        on trees

Beavers at Bantam

Dragging our kayaks
into the water

we search
for just the right
time

the edge of dusk
or dawn

It's hit
or miss

but it's worth
trudging
over the dams

just to have them
surround me

swimming
with such purpose

beady eyes
and big black noses
pressing forward

till suddenly
they realize
we're there

What's magic
to me
may be mundane

but the shocking
slap-diving
smack

sends chills
right through me

The Find

There's a sign
for *Sessions Woods*

off busy Route 69

just a name
not a place
till today

Following Beaver Pond Trail
past birthing skunk cabbage
unfurling huge ribbons
of green-yellow leaves
by the stream
in the shadow of trees

walking up and down hills
past meadow and woods

finding swamp
and beaver pond
spiked with dead trees
lilies afloat
green buds beneath water
so clear
tinted brown

moving on
from Monet

never dreaming
there could be more

a Japanese image appears

A sheer veil of water
glistening
falls from above
onto mossy green rocks
filling pools

spilling over
and into
my world

My Jungle

I'm tasting
the succulent
sweetness
of summer-sodden
air

Water's sluicing
'round rocks

With lion's roar
the river
held back
pounces over the dam

and I

am willing prey

The Point

From inside
my window
lifting weights
with a view

I feel
the fool

watching
the river's flow

Waist deep
fly-fisherman
fish

their voices
echoing calm

I wish

To Be There

Confused in Collinsville

The Axe Factory buildings
are waiting in vain
to be saved

Crumbling remnants
of what was once true
still echo
beating
trip-hammer tunes

This town's confused

Once humble
now quaint

it reinvents

But restaurants
boutiques
the bicycle trail

pale beside
the demise
of its heart

Steam Room Reverie

From the ceiling
swollen drops
of condensation
fall

I drift
into forests of rain
where orchids
flow freely
and essence
of green
envelopes the air

till the slam of the door
A new bather enters

My jungle
turns into
four walls

Homesteading

Florida's Highway
pulls us
past
aquas
and pinks

into Hurricane Andrew's wake

and we rubberneck
through Homestead

past
black words sprayed
on broken house billboards

STATE FARM
SUCKS

TRESPASSERS
WILL BE SHOT

Dead-end streets
their mouths agape
are missing random teeth

Dwellings
raw
stripped of skin
are dotted
with stacks of new shingles

Stucco villas
spew their guts
in heaps upon the pavement

shattered cribs
tables
toilets
toys

Just Another Intermission

from a CNN report on Bosnia

Toppled
church spires
stab the ground

Shattered
blood-stained glass
reflects

the fears
of the innocent

Stumbling on English
the priest
translates the scene

Silent

the camera tells more

scanning

lifeless
bullet-scarred streets

hungry women and children
huddled inside

daring to peek
from their doorways

Newsworthy

Glibly
we scan
the morning news
fingers flipping
through pages

our eyes
immune
to headlines

sipping coffee
nibbling toast
in the winter warmth
of our home

There's nothing
important
in the news
today

That is

unless
you're there

Ending a New York Love Affair

Once it was safe
for young girls
to travel on subways

and stand at stage doors
waiting
for glimpses of stars

Fantasies
sparkled
      and danced
            down the avenues

Now
crushed glass
tin cans
spittle
and pee

glitter
under streetlamps

Broadway is a beacon
illuminating lies
that hid in sidewalk cracks
while I was young

The city night stalks me
I run

past hollow desperate eyes
and open palms

The acrid stench
of soot
grabs hold

and I struggle
to give up my dreams

City Roots

I used to have to go
with others
Now
I can go alone

to claim this city
as my own

With every step
roots
reconnect

Once willow
now oak
I reach

toward musky roasted
chestnut smoke
mysteries of art at The Met
a cappella street songs
vendors hawking shawls

All the years
spent elsewhere
help me
see
how firmly
planted here

I'll always be

Before the Feast

for Daddy

I was barely ten
when I found a friend
at 70th and Fifth

The Frick

where for his dissertation
my dad dissected Duccio

while wandering the galleries
I discovered art

We practically lived there
for a year while he wrote

The guards all knew my name

I was the Eloise
of the museum

her Plaza Hotel
meager digs

Sir Thomas Moore
was watching
having eyes
only for me

The girl with the pearl earring
shimmering in light
whispered
confiding
Her secrets were mine

These paintings

hors d'oeuvres
for the feast
of my life

Through Brussels to Bruegel

Each week
a magnet pulls me
to the Museum of Ancient Art

past lacy architecture

guiding me
'round gothic spires
down cobbled paths
and through the doors

right into the painting
of carnival

where I slip through cracks
on dark glossy paint

seeking out
red-orange-green
wicked deeds

lascivious dancing
and ale

gambling
feasting
and brawling

animals mingling with men
people in trees and on rooftops
enthralled by the scene

I'm watching the devil cavorting
near saints

dreading
the magnet's release

based on Bruegel's painting "The Kermess"

Byzantine Eyes

for Joe

I remember Ravenna
its dim-shadowed chapel

where gilded mosaics
grabbed specks of light
for sparkle

and Byzantine eyes'
huge
almond orbs

loomed from above

Every time
I look at him
I see those eyes

peering out
from the present

connecting it
to the past

Bartholomew's Cobble

Ashley Falls, Massachussetts

I'm in the habit
of studying paintings
not being in them

but when I go
to Bartholomew's Cobble
brushstrokes
cover my skin

as I walk
the rocky knoll
that opens
into meadows
hayfields
pastures
of grazing cows

and weeping trees
leaning
towards the river's
ancient curves

An antique home
stands guard

Surely
Gainsborough's
been here

Jumieges

Wandering the countryside
I stumbled upon ruins

piles
of ancient crumbling stone

towering walls
enveloped
in green overgrowth

roofless

no altar

no pews

Grass grew
where monks
priests
parishioners
once stood

Blossoming white
tangling vines
filled empty arched window frames

As I gazed
from within
this peeled-open cathedral

God poured down
on the rays of the sun

Asana

Sanskrit for "pose"

It's that cabin fever
time of year

Needing more
than a treadmill
facing a wall

I take myself
to the trail

to view hints
of history
where train whistles
once blew

letting snowflakes
melt
in my hair
and tasting them
on my tongue

Others walk
with i-pods

I'm tuned

into earth and sky
the rustling of
hungry hawks
in the trees

the sound
of scrunching snow

My mind's
in a yoga pose

OTHER LIVES

Words for an Abuser

based on a news photo

Don't look at me
or point your lens
hiding
in cowardly safety

Crouched
in this corner
hugging myself

I am
my own gift

whose arms
will not unwrap
for you

the softness
that yours
have misshapen

Healing beneath
my own trusted fingers

I'll choose
when and how
to unveil
my new strength

and be gone
from your picture
forever

Through the Wringer

Her fabric
is limp
and faded
      hanging on the line
fibers frayed gray
exposed to the wind

that seeks
and finds
her weakness

sifting itself
      through
           invisible
                holes
where washboards
and words
had their way

Worlds Removed

Far from her familiar world
my mother sat on the Mississippi train
watching a young woman board
A tiny sack
of skin and bones
        hanging limply
            from her arms
                whimpering
as in reflex
she swayed
to the beat

Her thin
worn
empty
pale face
lost
between drooping straw hat
and shapeless red hillbilly dress

had withdrawn from a world
whose cries
she could no longer hear

Bringing Her Back

after "Memories" by Norman Rockwell

She's old
wrapped in shawls
folds of orange
deep green
and collared in lace

Memory's brightening
the fade in her eyes

as she sits
on a stool
in the attic

surrounded
by photos and artifacts

The soldier
framed and covered in glass
leans up against ceiling beams

his letter dangling
from her hand
at arm's length

Averting her gaze
she travels
somewhere else

Round and Round

with thanks to Gail

All dressed up
clutching her purse
she sits
on the carousel seat

From her throne
she waves
again and again
to an audience of none

with childlike smiles

her age defying all

wrinkled
bent over
joy
in her eyes

Lost to the present
found in the past

she spins
with calliope sounds

Friday After School

She turns the key
        pressing her exhaustion
                against the opening door

                        Emptiness sucks her in

She hears the echo
of her heel and toe
tapping on tile

                Gravity
                      pulls her
                            into a chair

A newspaper
finds her fingers
but the words are lost

Others' needful children
become a background hum

the pain
        from her own life
staccato

Like the pummeled
tightly stretched skin
of a drum

her center   is worn thin

They Will Be Watching

Children unheard

cowering
cringing
wondering what's wrong

exhausted
from trial and error

dragging
their broken questions

sinking
in purple-tinged shadows

hiding fears
in fantasy

they recede into walls
become one with walls

The venom and shouting
bounce off them

Shards of shattered plates
nick them

Someday
they'll emerge
to replay the scene

and the walls
the walls
will be watching

Their Turn

The air
is sodden sponge

yet summertime's splashing

Slippery bodies
are skidding on grass

There's giggling

Water's dribbling
from the hose

Wilting
I watch
blossoming childhood

take its turn

Almost

Unembellished
dressed
in black

firmly
gently
they massage
my neck and hands

pushing
twisting
rolling thumbs
into palms
and pressure points

slippery
laced with lotion
milking fingers
like teats

painting my nails
with the richness of red

An intimate connection

till buzzing
the timer goes off

and I pay

Tuned into the Harp

*James Montgomery–Infinity Hall,
Norfolk, Connecticut, April 2010*

He takes the stage
tall and skinny
dressed in black
Swivel hips
swiftly sway

Caressing the mouth harp
mic in hand

flailing arms
kicking feet
whipping the cord

he's possessed
if not by God
then by music
born again

Blues become the man

Bowing down
into wailing sounds
then rising
bending backwards
he brings down the house

His fluttering hands
beckon the band
but he plays the audience too

strutting backwards and forwards
slowing then halting
teasingly
bringing us back

till the set
is done

The encore comes

He blows
the walls
apart

Misjudging Jo

She started out
as sandpaper

her voice
scraping
our uneasy skins

Perfectly overdressed

angular jewelry
make-up armor

lipstick
sharply
defining her edges

Her lizard tongue
lashed out
at life

but
she listened
to us all

In turn
we offered trust

till
she finally
cried
her soft insides
out

More Than a Boss

to Von

She enters
the room
creating the space
then bursts
out of its seams

Admiration
shock
belly laughter
follow
in her wake

Her kindness
wraps
around our need

Familiar Faces

The Potter's Hands

Years haven't dulled the sting of anticipation

I see each black hair
sprouting
from my father's weathered olive skin

flat nails
       crusted white

outspread fingers

tendons strung tensely

          poised

                   for slow-motion slaps

those hands
       that hovered large
before my child eyes

hands
   whose palms
       molded spinning clay
          into pots
             full of fear

But I was made of different clay
              and hid from the potter's wheel

While waiting
           for those fingers and palms
to find me

      I hardened
to stone

To Be Clay

My father
lived life
all ups and downs

His moods
ruled our days

A child
dressed up
as a man

he knew how to play

Without him
fun's
no longer
the same

He had such gifts
to share

but fear and uncertainty
turned me to stone

He was joy
He was rage

I'm so glad
that sometimes

I chose
to be clay

When We Communed

My father
talked incessantly
and wore Hawaiian shirts

He engulfed
and embarrassed
us all

except
when we went fishing

The rocking motions
of the boat
and the soil-scent
of baited hooks

transformed him

Sunshine
and salt air
were enough

We sat in perfect silence
dropping our lines
waiting
for our poles to bend

Best Week of the Year

We weren't exactly poor
Our parents put money aside
for the one week
we went away
to New Hampshire

I remember
the first time
as we approached
the mountains
and thought
they were clouds

the general store
with the chiseled
wooden Indian
standing outside

where we reveled
in the purchase
of penny candy

the bumpy
terrifying ride
as our tiny
mint-green
station wagon
hurtled
down the rock strewn
vertical path

to the house
on Lake Winnipesaukee

Every year
when we arrived

Daddy and I
would abandon the car
and its contents

We'd toss off
our clothes
in the dark
and dive
from the dock

splashing
and laughing

My sister
and I
fished
with our father

We threaded
thick slimy worms
onto hooks
just to be with him

He'd take us all
to see the sights

He also rowed
beside me
as I proudly
swam
to the island
in the cove

At night
my sister and I

sinking
into feather pillows
and beds

whispered secrets
while listening
to loons

He Found a Way

Our apartment
was under
the subway el

The rattling
and roaring
shook the walls

We also lived
near the airport

Jets flew loudly
overhead
competing
with the trains

drowning out
Walter Cronkite
and telephone conversations

This
was our normal

So were the frequent
picnics
orchestrated
by my dad

He'd pack up
the family
and Popo
the dog
the hibachi
the ice chest
marshmallows
and steaks

Off to Long Island
we'd go
to Hecksher State Park

where he and I
would slide down
sand dune cliffs
each slippery grain
propelling us
past
tall tickling grasses
down to the shore

Then we'd climb
back up
for more

till finally we'd walk
along the beach
dig in the sand
search for shells

fire up the grill

sit side by side

listen
to the soft
sound
of waves

After the Funeral

Hollow
is this naked house

stripped bare
of him

of what was home

My father's gone

His hearth is cold

Beside his bed
an empty slipper
waits

The mold of a familiar shape
fills again

Out steps the man

To Be Heard

My father
was fun
cruelty
chaos

My mother
meek
a blank slate
was hardly ever heard

and hardly heard
what I had
to say

Now
that she's ninety-one
all veneer
stripped away

I offer her
hearing aids

"Why
would I
need them"
she asks

"when I already know
what I'm going
to say?"

The Hug

We had a history
of hands off
love

I never doubted
her
though I always
longed
for more

She
just couldn't
reach out
touch

her few kisses
checkmarks
on a chalkboard

She
grew up
without affection
and passed it along

Suddenly
in her old age
she resents
longs for
demands
what she never had
never gave

She watches
with envy
my warm embrace
of in-laws
friends
relatives

What feels
so free
so natural
with others

is forced
with us

Our hugs
are awkward squeezes
stiff
perfunctory
pats on the back

I try
but neither she
nor I
knows how

She's ninety-one
deserves
what she wants

I'd hoped
that fake
was enough

In My 45th Year

finally

she stood up
for me

This meek and timid
soul

rose

with hands
on hips
face red

Fierce words
from a place
unknown

nurtured me
with rage

She Was

Will I remember
just the forgetting

not the fierceness
of hands on hips

her meekness
morphed
into mother bear

not the gentle control
of family turmoil
with a look

not the sweet soprano
of kitchen sink songs

but the scratchy
record-skipped stories
instead

This onetime
giver
of succor

is shuffling
dwindling
shriveling

into a dot

small as the details
of daily life

She suffocates
us
while surrounding
herself

with the safety
of sameness

She's gone

Miriam

    a handful of people   a life full of love
    the casket is lowered   solid and strong
    with no rabbi present   beliefs were her own
    such emptiness   there was warmth

    just a few words   meanings were clear
    simply spoken   there was trust

    as the dirt's tossed   her being surrounds us
    rain melts the sky   with flashes of memory

    her death's an aside   life goes on

    with too few
    to remember
    her gifts

Mother-in-Law

With her
imposing stature
commanding voice

such a presence

she either charms
or offends

There's no telling
when
she'll try
to engage
unsuspecting strangers
in conversation

unaware

or perhaps
not caring
to read
their faces

Impatient
short
she blurts

but
she goes
out of her way

for others
never waiting
to be asked

She's the heart
pumping life
into
our family

She's shrunk
several inches
in recent years

Now
we see
eye to eye

Finally

I can tell her
exactly
what I think

that I love her

The Circle

for Chuck

Filled
    with overflow
        of life
our bicycle
    thickly spills
        to the ground
clumsy
    loving
        laughter
tipsy
    and twisted
        within the spokes

From down
        the foggy cobbled way
an old man appears

Wistfully smiling
        watching us
he whispers
    "I too was once young"

Louvain, Belgium, early 1970's

His Morning Detail

for Chuck

The alarm
rings in daybreak
and minutes
of lingering silence
are his

There's a sureness
in his shedding of sheets
and in his feet
touching carpet

The rhythm
of morning
begins
as he carefully
switches on
hidden lights
trying
not to disturb me

but I groggily worship
his waking

the quick squeak
of faucet
and hissing of shower
streaming
over his body

the thwack
of wet towel
against flesh

the coarse stroke
of bristles
on scalp

I love the dull clatter
of shaving cream can
the slippery scrape
of blade upon beard
and the flicking
of water
from fingers

Now the padding of feet
has a more wakeful sound
each step
pressing deeply
with purpose

I hear the click-swishing
of hangers and clothes

the silk-sliding tones
of his tie

the rustle
of jacket

pulled over
broad shoulders

Soon his weight
tips the edge
of the mattress
There's a tugging
and prickling
of socks
catching the hairs
on his shins

He rises
to reach
the dresser
For an instant
change jingles
then solidly
clanks
into pants-pocket place

Pencils and pens
rattle and clink
as they're gathered
against his chest

His watch band
swings
then snaps shut

Rolling over
in bed
crumpling blankets and sheets

I muffle
the sounds
of his leaving

The Affair

In every other way
though it's cliché
he is the perfect husband

I really shouldn't complain

especially since
I'm so high maintenance

He deserves
a reprieve

It began
seven years ago

innocently

I knew
all about it

I forgave

I decided
open marriage
has its place

But it's getting old

I'm envious
of the time

they spend together

He's only mine
during bad weather

I get tossed
the scraps
of time

All balance
is off

Hoping
to maintain
the status quo

he refuses to see

he's chosen
the golf course
over me

For Isabella

She loves
the tickles
begs for more

I adore
the husky chortle
reverberating
from
her tiny being

and those pouty lips
spouting
perfect imperfections

Blonde hair
blue eyes
in a cherub's face
so out of place
with my roots

But
I feel
my blood
pulsing
through her

She's the precious part
of what her parents
once had

Her foundation's
been shattered

We fill
the cracks
with love

Selective Memories

for Daniel

My most fragile
baby bird
so knobbledy-legged
is chirping
and cheeping
fear and delight

Wildly
he pumps
and overtakes
the flock

Cocky
standing up
pushing
on the pedals
rattling chains
he whirs
up-down hills

till forgetting
his newness of skill
I steer him astray
suggesting
he look
at the view

Turning his head
and handlebars
he veers wildly
off the path
bumping downhill
towards a tree

After
the crash
there is silence

While waiting
long seconds
for breath
to return
he pushes
my comfort
away

Will his memories
be of flight
or of falling

Mine
are of
his trembling
sparrow bones

Now That He's Back

I grieved
six years
for his missing
future

He tried
to get on
with his life

finished college

while disease
lay in wait

Suddenly
a biopsy's
come back normal

The chess board's
been changed

Expectations
are back
in play

Trying to find
a new strategy

I ruffle
his feathers
for a reaction
but he works
in his own time
not mine

baking
and cooking
with abandon

no thoughts
of health
or function

Now
that he's back
I coddle
too much

but how
could I not

though he
keeps
a certain distance

The truth
is I coddled
before
he was sick

Different
an outsider

always
a loner
though not
by choice

he was sweet
smart
and funny
with us

No longer ill
there's something
still fragile
about him

my grown-up child

I can't
help him

find his life

Salt on Ice

for Jesse

I curdle when I hear
his name
I turn his photos around

I run errands
I prepare the meals

but he slips through fissures
in my calm

Salt
is all
I taste
since I've sent him away

On the phone
I hear my voice
clipped
and cold
as it greets
his warm ramblings

His hopes
bounce off
a frozen shield

that will melt
when he comes home

Leah's Timeless Face

Swiftly unsnarling tangles
caught in present time

I'm rhythmically twisting
and weaving
her glossy chestnut mane

braiding
spiral curls
from centuries past

Beneath my hands
a Botticelli face
peers out

and the background fades
to a gilded frame
upon a museum wall

As It Must Be

for my children, Jesse, Leah and Daniel

I want
to give
the empty nest
cliché
a rest

but

I remember
the book
I read
to you
over
and over
again

Where is my mother
the little chick cried

Where is she now
Where will she be

Roles
are unraveling

Weathered twigs
fall to the ground

As I mother
my mother
my little chicks
no longer cry
for me

About the Author

Joan B. Kantor was born and raised in New York City, whose cultural richness has been a great source of inspiration. She graduated from Queens College with a Bachelor's Degree in History and Education and then went on to live and teach in Europe for seven years, where she traveled extensively. After receiving her Master's Degree from Antioch University, Joan became a learning disability specialist and counselor at Manchester Community College, where she continues to work. Married to her high school sweetheart, she has three grown children and a granddaughter. She currently lives on the Farmington River in the charming village of Collinsville, Connecticut. Joan's passions for people, nature, traveling and the arts merge in the poetry that she has been writing for most of her life. She has been published in *ByLine, Chadder,* and *Namaste.*

This book is set in Garamond Premier Pro, which had its genesis in 1988 when type-designer Robert Slimbach visited the Plantin-Moretus Museum in Antwerp, Belgium, to study its collection of Claude Garamond's metal punches and typefaces. During the mid-fifteen hundreds, Garamond—a Parisian punch-cutter—produced a refined array of book types that combined an unprecedented degree of balance and elegance, for centuries standing as the pinnacle of beauty and practicality in type-founding. Slimbach has created an entirely new interpretation based on Garamond's designs and on comparable italics cut by Robert Granjon, Garamond's contemporary.

To order additional copies of this book
or other Antrim House titles, contact the publisher at

Antrim House
21 Goodrich Rd., Simsbury, CT 06070
860.217.0023, AntrimHouse@comcast.net
or the house website (www.AntrimHouseBooks.com).

•

On the house website
are sample poems, upcoming events,
and a "seminar room" featuring supplemental biography,
notes, images, poems, reviews, and
writing suggestions.